Also by Michael Boughn

Poetry:

Iterations of the Diagonal (*shuffaloff*, 1995)

Dislocations in Crystal (Coach House Books, 1998)

22 Skidoo/SubTractions—Opus Minus One (Book Thug, 2009)

Cosmographia—A Post-Lucretian Faux Micro-Epic (Book Thug, 2010)

Nine Blue Moments for Robin (BlazeVox, 2012)

Great Canadian Poems for the Aged—Vol. 1, Illus. Ed. (Book Thug, 2013)

City—A Poem from the End of the World (Spuyten Duyvil, 2016)

Hermetic Divagations—After H.D. (Spuyten Duyvil, 2018)

Uncertain Remains (BlazeVox, 2022)

Prose:

Into the World of the Dead—Astonishing Adventures in the Underworld (Annick Press, 2006)

Business as Usual, A Novel (NeWest Press, 2011)

Measure's Measures—Literary Assays (Station Hill Press, 2022)

Editor:

H.D.—A Bibliography 1905-1990 (University Press of Virginia, 1993)

The H.D. Book, by Robert Duncan, with Victor Coleman (University of California Press, 2011)

Resist Much, Obey Little—Inaugural Poems for the Resistance (with 18 others) (Spuyten Duyvil, 2017)

Narthex and Other Stories by H.D. (Book Thug, 2011)

Dispatches from the Poetry Wars, with Kent Johnson (2016-2020)
archived at the Contemporary Literature Collection,
Simon Fraser University Library Special Collections

THE BOOK OF UNCERTAIN

**

A HYPERBIOGRAPHICAL USER'S MANUAL

BOOK ONE

Michael Boughn

SPUYTEN DUYVIL

New York City

Some of these poems have appeared previously in *Dispatches from the Poetry Wars*, *Touch the Donkey*, the chapbook *The Book of Uncertain [Leaving]* (BullHead 2017), and in various versions in *Uncertain Remains* (BlazeVox 2022).

© 2022 Michael Boughn

ISBN 978-1-956005-68-4

cover art: t thilleman

Library of Congress Cataloging-in-Publication Data

Names: Boughn, Michael, author.
Title: The book of uncertain : a hyperbiographical user's manual / Michael
Boughn.
Description: New York City : Spuyten Duyvil, [2022] | Series: A
hyperbiographical user's manual ; book 1
Identifiers: LCCN 2022034332 | ISBN 9781956005684 (paperback)
Subjects: LCGFT: Poetry.
Classification: LCC PR9199.4.B68 B66 2022 | DDC 811/.6--dc23/eng/20220721
LC record available at https://lccn.loc.gov/2022034332

"You cannot be certain about uncertainty."
— Frank Knight, *Risk, Uncertainty, and Profit*

"The poem: a prolonged hesitation between sound and sense."
— Paul Valéry, *Tel Quel*

CHAPTER ONE

Leaving

CHAPTER TWO

Some simplified examples of chaos

CHAPTER THREE

Etiquette lesson #1: possible responses to improper uncertain advances

CHAPTER 4

The pragmatics of to belong as not belonging
—uncertain ontological whims and communal phantasies

CHAPTER 5

Uncertain Taxonomies of Uncertain

CHAPTER SIX

Interlinear to some simplified examples of chaos

CHAPTER SEVEN

A Methodology for Verifying Fugitive Apparitions in Uncertain Glances

CHAPTER 8

Gluten free pornography, myth, and your health

CHAPTER 9

Introduction to random

CHAPTER 10

Leaving 2 Including a special section on Leaving Art

LEAVING

with thanks to Branka Arsić

Three categories of leaving

often overlooked in the rush

to get started:

> dreaming

> > thinking

> > > loving

> > > There are others

equally composed of phonemic jiggling

and they, too, are overlooked

from great heights where Uncertain appears

ant-like in their midst

> Shopping

> > for instance

> > > which recent developments

in ontological terraforming

have rendered central to a range

of gestures reformulated in the likeness

of *not* leaving

Dreaming, thinking, and loving are not

pushovers in anyone's book, especially

this one, indicating that what does not change

will leave

       It will leave you with a strange feeling

in the pit of your belly and it will

leave unintended consequences to play out

in the lives of multitudes as they

leave for work at 6 AM

headed south

for a fiery crash on the 400

               They dreamt

of flames last night, and

tatters fluttered in morning's mirrored eyes

but they left anyway, then Armageddon

Dreaming, thinking and loving may require

further registers of reception if they

mean to configure present

considerations of serious investments

in Uncertain

Leaving, demonologically inflected

is sometimes confused with believing

not unlike the will to leave and will leave

There you have it, leaving

or meeting, say, Harvey, which was not

auspicious but leads to Harvey emerges

onto the grid from silent mountains
Lightbearer
carrying light to Buffalo and points

south and west, invisible to panoptical apparati

tracking excessive and unregistered aberrations

in the system's message delivery components
                                        Let's eat

he'd say, paying for all, an Angel

of circulation, "that rare being,"

Dorn said, "who made you feel

intensely alive"

It's not certain

that leaving is an adumbration

of conditions akin to breathing

or peeing, but evidence suggests a long

history where history reeks

of inconsequential foliation

of millennial population flow

across the front yard of elusive monuments

wretched remnants

of distanced halves

Uncertain

formulas for breaching confidence

leave little room to wiggle in the face

of shopping extravaganza's ever ready

not to be missed

half-price Sale

of the Century

Leaving the Centre is not easy

with just two decades of minutes

to lean on, but a kind of inevitable

graduation from grandfather and uncles

cleaning guns at the picnic, sun glint off blue

oiled steel lights talk of war's constant

subaudible wounds never far from mind

Gassed in the trenches

shot on the beach, beat

in the kitchen, fucked

by the old man, war

rages, beckons through and beyond

domestic brutality, deep tonality

a beloved rupture rolling

through faded streets evaporate

in time's flood, deco curves, once

upon a time care lost to dust and heat

                              Leaving is that quick

the desert slips into dream form

the road winds by torrents through gaps

in the peaks till the din of war dims

and the border looms

                    Mourning

is leaving's repressed signature

its uncertain step toward

distant crest, quivering gold leaf

to the light of another sunrise on the Bay

or grey layered fading into distances

of misted self

      First the death of water, sickly gray

      green slime, nitrogen blooms

                      Then falls

      No, then music

      but not here, not from here

      not exactly music

      but as close as a word can come

      to joy of knows something

      called *living water,* then

      falls. No, then climbs

      up, as if no question of up

      was issued, of course it was up then

      falls and some hitting

      till final earth spreads away

      pebbles an inexplicable order

      of shattered meaning

                    Falls in love

          is an *ekstasis* of helpless abandon

          as falls apart acknowledges

          uncertain depths of together

            Falls asleep ups the ante

          with dreams.

            Falls out of a tree

          pursuing angelic choir leaves

          uncertain in hands beyond shakes

          or lives as if *in the hands of*

          is the measure of knows

Dreaming, thinking, and loving fall

with persistent rhythms infiltrate

uncertain directions to the refuge

long felt to nestle among peaks

recede in shades of grey on grey, dove

grey, the greys of stones tumbled

on the Pleistocene beach, ashes

If loving is leaving

    what's gained adds up to an incurable

    distance of ashes between moments of lost

    sums, a spacing of intricacies

    entangled in a web of thinking

    beyond *mine*

Leaving as falling is a trope too far

its sleazy unconditional transitions

slip between levels of informational

intersection
        Grandfather's

and uncle's talk of wounds, their

oily blue steel flashes as someone cranks

the ice cream maker, steps

on a hot butt flipped carelessly

into the grass, sign of uncertain

family connections which lacking

ordinary forgiveness miss

love's uncertain connections

fade into smog

Harvey leaves the mountains

enters the grid, bears Light

of leaving, of breached

rule, picks apples and sells

joy at a fair price right across

the myth, follows paths

of mound building Indians in the map

made out of thin air, jazz

love of unearthed fact

beneath the asphalt—flips through the albums

till Craig Harris, *Black*

Bone, says is this yours?

and everything's alright, bathed

in music's forgiveness, generosity

of unforeseen channels of circulation

flow through peaks and by torrents

across borders of formidable

interdimensional accumulated

greed presses against leaving

Chapter Two
Some simplified examples of chaos

Moving on, chaos announces

a break in the text

      It's not that

leaving is over, but its uncertain

resolution begs for nuance

leads to other eruptions

        until information

and transformation verge on *sheer*

acoustic focus and forget to mean

the usual bullshit

      That said

three or more objects in a solar system

lead to orbital chaos

not to mention microcracks

and atomic scale dislocations

though its turbulent heart predictably

stalls in a river of sluggish red lights

on the way home at 6

Home

is not a strange attractor, tho it

may be a simplified example of chaos

burns through a case

of Early Times each week

three sheets to *home* and oblivion's

tender kiss in the wreckage

America scattered among smudge

pots, littered on the beach

at the end of that long, bloody

destiny manifested finally

in Black Friday's furious

shopping chaos

And bodies heaped

in War's corners,

where children bleed

in bombed out remains

of various agreements

Late night border glare, electric

interrogation, examination

and release into passage down

darkened Granville into blank

city at world's edge, weed

brownies gone, destination a chance

flyer picked up in a random diner

on the road north to a rumoured

mythology of water ups the ante

with 45 days and 45 nights

of rain leave the world

steaming in merciful light

breaks through to shine on

                          chaos of war

that followed through streets

distant from bloody encounters

a chaos of sudden resistance

within larger chaos, surging bodies

fists feet screams

cop's skittering gun across asphalt

into the night

Another simplified example of chaos

Logos as click-bait indicates

good for a nickel regardless

of consequent darkness unleashed

at its most nasty might bring

to the dance, heart beat

                     of eroding human

crumbles, blown away

you could say by

the winds of time if you had

the guts

        Blame it on Pablo or Gertrude

chasm crossed or maybe

entered, such clear directions being

first past the post that leaves them

behind

        Chaos complicates

enters the lexicon in alt-formation's

post-truth reality shows'

deft manipulation of exorbitant

cruelty and humiliation,

democracy's final card, its

levelling spirit's malevolent

grip on human's last common

decency intent to impose really mean

Father Knows Best rerun lockup

configurations on civilization as we

know it

      Or say *knew*, since the question

having been begged

leaves a wake of confusion, a sign

of distraught Time

> *It became clear to me that they view jobs as lollipops, things you give out to good boys and girls, instead of the sense that actually what you're trying to do is recruit the best possible talent to fill the most important, demanding, lowest-paying executive jobs in the world.*
>
> —Eliot Cohen on President-elect Trump's appointments

      It keeps coming back to lollipops

      frivolous quip acquired from the new

      order of business emerges from the Protestant

      Mean Streak Ed Sanders named

      ascendant under the sign of Death

      all along

John Winthrop

barely able to contain his glee

at the news—*licentious* Anne Hutchinson

who had cast off ordinances and churches

and her children

Anne, William, Katherine, Mary, Zariel

scalped and burned in a bloody heap

and Winthrop, sweaty with the news

going all *Trump that bitch*, dreaming

of lollipops, the line of supplicants

stretching down City's hill

around the block, all the way

to the golf club, a worm-like

spontaneous self-revelation

lollipops providing *the amateurs of hell*

a system to shape hate into visible

formations intent on extending control

over the doctrine of grace and any

other perceived aberration from

their Doom Program while eliminating

façades of compassion and even

bureaucratic compassion control

mechanisms to get down

to Business

Somewhere something

gyres and *slouches*, something stirs

and drags its slimy ass up 5th Avenue

straightens its power tie, buttons

its jacket, shines its assortment

of time tested cruelties, waiting

to be offered a lollipop, shouting its

commitment to keep on Trumping

the Bitch who now has become upper

case in a gesture extends Her significance

beyond The Tower into domains

of *touch* and *welcome*, *care* and the querulous

eyes of kids

caught in the slaughter

(*for Ed Sanders*)

Small examples of chaos are a dime a dozen in post-apocalyptic
fantasies of deranged divine etymologies for lack of an elusive
word designating shadow mirrored in the drama of yet anoth-
er arrangement of imprisoned exigencies. Sometimes it says it
without you

Sometimes it says it without you and all you can do is watch
you could say in horror though then the shadow of doubt is
beyond the pale and misses more familiar dislocated encounters

The Central Committee dreams itself in broken sleep, depos-
its small examples of chaos resemble the United MiStake of
Amerika among mass graves yet to be recovered from amnesia
induced indifference to everything but *football* and *lock and load*
could be its moral imperative chaotically circulating in min-
iscule invasions through grand halls gilded with the tortured
ground of empires past

    Chaos goes both ways and the ride

    reeks meaning riven flashes

    motherfather wounds ooze

    sexy Splendor in the Orange

    Grove vibes, an inheritance guaranteed

    by universal agreement

    that *Indians* (not the cool ones

    from the movies like Apaches

    or Commanches but generic

no name *Indians*) just *adored* building

those quaint Missions designed

to obliterate them body and soul, a literal

planned and executed *reduction*

to pave the way for good Christian Mega-Malls

and a Freeway System approaches

the complexity of the unsalvaged

human soul going and coming

amid the ruins of love

awaits its Dreamer

        Harvey jumps the gun, exits

        the mountains in a whirlwind of light

        shreds the ranks of days, Ornette wailing

        new sonic prophecies leave chaos

        stunned and confused as to its

        prospects in post partum regime

        of the *mysterium*

                Leaving shows up

as foretold in alignments

of Taurean determined refusal

to accept war as the natural outcome

of maternal infidelities and prosperity's

stupefaction

      Chaos then looks like home

where home, rigid with rage, sacrifices

children to names desire throws up

in convulsed fatherly violence

and the legacy of her daddy's lust

      leaves mum to stagger

      from cock to cock's unmitigated

      pain, empty

        At the border mountains announce

        the end of the world where chaos dwells

        in catastrophe and catastrophe

        names unfolding road through dissonance

        sounding how many enemies

        make a soul

            Dictation slashes

the darkness

            Wars sing out

civilization's credo

                Harvey

holds steady

Step right up, getcher tickets to the gold-plated

End of the World, now appearing daily, America's new

favourite past time, Ascendent Darkness

of the Whoop Ass CEOs. Watch them bend the world

over a barrel while chanting Drill, baby, drill,

as optional ethics and alternate facts

convene in the basement, stumble through pizza

boxes and Rose Bowl echoes in sepulchral

halls of the Republic's razzle dazzle

death rattle. Fun while it lasted

but when the party's over it's time

to sell the works. If it doesn't sell

apply lipstick and a slinky dress

well-padded with Slovenian silicone

and Russian intelligence. The market

will bear whatever gold-plated delusions

pledge allegiance to end's shill

War's chaos is not part of its prosaic

declaration of allegiance remains

to be seen in relics of shuttered

mind's ineluctable modalities

of bone

        is a new

mythology of water standing naked

defiant, before her burning home

puckered flesh aglow in flame lit

hieroglyphic histories of terror

and refusal's interminable next

shimmer

        War is the name of burning

and home seduces it, a chaos

of strange desire out of the war

and into the mountains

reeks of chaosophically dissolved

orders of already finished outsets

Whose body of knowledge arches

in pleasure of unlawful carnal

relation is a matter of no small

significance

       Or stakes it down

beat it into submission

          The masques

of love, soaked in bourbon

and anger, stiffen, split

fall away

      To shed is to say

love is a derelict salt mine

After the end is over, chaos becomes known

as a common stake, a familiar figure in local

dives, sighted frequently at inaugural

moment's repeated threat to launch regimes

of pure greed exorbitant even

by 2008 standards in tough talking

homage to ancient thunder god's

thoughtful contribution to yet another

bloody holocaust

Pieces of flesh accumulate

between the poem's words, the casual

collateral damage of God's

impossible name

　　　　　Boundaries fade to between

night and day or day and night

revelation's nursey breeches

chaos in shades of turquoise

and heavy indeterminate

light

　　　　　Then it wavers, leaving's dream

rolling dice in doorway out a bus

window, seven come eleven, boxcars

snake eyes, arrival's vernacular

departure where unsettled turn

leads

Finding a simplified example of chaos

is harder than you'd think given general level

of mindlessness driven at the moment

by a yellow haired, orange skinned simulacrum

You're here

till you're not

so you'd think

the taste of carrots

and other ineffable

breezes across the soul

not to mention sustaining necessity

of kindness to others in same sinking

boat would count

Chaos evades

the equation, erupts in a black mask

hurling fiery bottles at random signs

of its rage writ in neon

while *untranslatable transitory* dances

around the conflagration

Deterministic chaos offers another entry

into subjective commensurations

of these strange days

when chaos runs amok

and trillions are a stake

through the heart

of uncertain

Somewhere

something's

hay

wire

shadows crawling out

to foul air with stench

of cupidity, so that even

the obvious pun has no room

to stretch out, contraction

having left intelligence to inhabit

a nasty toolbox of tyrannical brays

    But compound pendula

    measles epidemics and irregular

    chicken hearts assert independence

    of declaration free ends

                  The gun skitters

    across the poem into the night, electrifies

    the City anticipates chaos as war

    spreads through its nerves

Abstract

fumes of children's burning flesh

sponsored by American Industry

and the Terror Progress leave

multitudes of consumers unsure

which sale to attend first

Since they are simplified examples

uncertain rain forests refuse to populate

adumbrations of their exemplary

syntax

One word after another

is not always enough, although in this case

it does get across the border

Harvey waits, unsure

what the poem wants from him

as light fades, as then

and now stagger, no longer

capable of rational insurrection

fall into a torpor of indistinguishable

battles whose bodies pile up

in pits dug from the lexical

substratum where *artillery*

and *band* are stencilled across

the ruins of music, or at least

music's *that way,* holds the host

to its brutal advance beyond

this way

　　　Simplified examples

of chaos abound in complex

microstructures of phase space

but refuse ulterior reassignment

Having nothing to say

is no reason not to say it

with heart

CHAPTER THREE
ETIQUETTE LESSON #1: POSSIBLE RESPONSES TO IMPROPER UNCERTAIN ADVANCES

With thanks to Ludwig Wittgenstein for the certainty

It's tough starting out after chaos

initiated incursions into otherwise

stable reconfigurations

of leaving

       The War

drags on, sends Images

             a flaming girl

             her mouth

             a dark hole

             of excruciating intimacy

with Uncertain's interruptions

of perennial thought of connection's

fundament which sometimes stands

for anatomy but also looks

like a napalmed rice paddy

[But even if in such cases I

can't be mistaken

isn't it possible

that I am drugged?]

                    Bear with me

then breaches normal poetic

protocol's insistent eruption

of lyric diversions and faith-based

self-mutilation to face the music

screeching out of the meeting

of commerce and community

                         No way around

that one, ragged across the sidewalk

huddled on a grate

Uncertain advances dissolve

typical desolation issues

in a puppy's dream whimper,

in the furnace of leaving

that is not leaving and not

just for beginning

There you have it, *Leaving*

It's well-known uncertain advances

come in different shapes

often unrecognizable

beneath tawdry finery

                    If confronted

or otherwise hailed by Uncertain

responding to gestures of lewd intent

may get you through the door

but guarantees are out

of the question

along with necessary answers

              For instance

          hawking commie papers

          at Bathurst and Bloor

to a chorus of enraged Hungarians,

grounds for advance in regimes

of certain flawless reason

        Behold

they clamour, shiny *Image* calling out

from truth's light

        while bodies

writhe beneath tracks of advancing

Edenic convulsions, good for what

ails ya in the theatre of flawless

binary extrapolation into life

or death abstraction and watertight

righteousness

        Back home, mothers

weep in the street

till the drugs kick in—

        Librium & Valium

        Angel's names pouring

                from oblivion's cornucopia

reeking of orange blossoms and endless

ease in unceasing sun's

lost connection to regimes

of shadow find their nook

in complicated exegetic crannies

in Contraction's wham bam

thank you ma'm rendition

of "Moonlight Becomes You"

The Names sing

of immanent rhythm, Jurupa

Magnolia, Brockton, Palm

resonant with the taste

of honeyed place, dream's

topography, desire's moist

passages, memory's thick

patina

      Is there a shrink in the 2nd

Ring of Hell for those whose Father left

them an insatiable wound?

                      Was that Eve's

hunger?

      Did Yahweh, wifeless, come

in the night, Almighty?

                  Darkness breeds

in relentless sunlight,

orange blossoms' cloying fragrance,

thick oily residue of the smudge

pots, crash of wave after wave

of Western Civ against the edge

Names recede in the rear

view mirror as *what's*

in a name is lost to noisy

border's blur

        New mythologies

of water tangled knots'

demand for sense struggles

behind improper advances

toward perfection's mean dream

                Mountains' promise

embraced in distance's familiar

further, finds itself at home

in a dark alley with nothing

but a 2x4 to get it through

        In cases of Internal Uncertain

        Executive Orders offer opportunity

        to fine tune malice, maximize

        chaos, and unleash your inner

        demon—First Rule: locate

        the weak, kick the living shit

        out of them

        is certain

This will encourage your average off

duty cop to grab a brown-skinned kid

off the street and in cases of outrageous

resistance pull the trigger

to punish the absence

of documented existence

while ensuring the Doom Program's

traffic simplification plan

can maximize the sale and use

of smart-ass-free real estate

sure of terror's welcome

                         Large scale

roundups follow, invoke teary

recollections of John Wayne

and Tyrone Power punching cows

across (recently) empty(ied) Vastness

subject to perusal from ridges

deemed musically fenceless

                                 Howling

at the moon remains optional

Rage ravaged days' face left

to stagger under War's burden

                    Screaming

Hungarians signal the universal

declaration of inflicted agony

remains in force

                    It was a grand old time

                                        Red

is the East rolled off our tongues

like *Polly Wolly Doodle* and running

dogs were subject to joyous

unrestrained abuse

                    Woof

woof they howled, whether

at the moon or not is a question

of verbal uncertain that later

investigation indicates

lacks deep understanding

of linguistic whimsy's *geo-genesis*

and *cosmo-diddly-do*

Just

when you think you got

the damn rules straight, *lady moon*

opens up *in sweet silence*

and uncertain advances vaporous

hieroglyphs across her face

> [*Here I am inclined to fight*
>
> *windmills, because I cannot*
>
> *say the thing*
>
> *I really want to say*]

In some circumstances uncertain advances may *call upon things to testify*

in their light. This is common and should not cause alarm. You may choose to address them in terms appropriate to the emitted spectrum, or simply to stare in unmediated wonder. Touching is permitted in the company of awe.

Having left is not leaving, however uncertain

the advance

Slipstreaming in the wake

of big rigs across the prairies because only

three cylinders are firing leaves you

behind, even with constant advance

Swapping cigarettes with young

Russian fishermen tied up at the docks

speaking only eyes and alien

noise leaves War in its wake

                              Wake

up terminates in sudden beach

steaming after the rains

                    The edge

of the world revisits Indo-European

habits, leaves them to lurch

toward a dénouement of uncertain

provenance

                    Just across English Bay

snow capped sentinels resist

further alliteration

                         Spirit bears

                    and Raven emerge, contest

subdivided devastation creeps

up mutilated flank but are trapped

and sold at ferry terminal

souvenir stands

Uncertain advances

resist, too, with tectonic shenanigans

accumulated micro-cracks

recall simple examples of chaos

increase appearance of coherence

but complicate calculations

of success

    Snow-capped sentinels

giggle at all the "c"s

        The poem shivers

Where does truth leave the crow

perched in leafless oak, intent

on her world?

        Meaning

buzzes beyond

traps laid by enemies

of difficulty in syntactic

lock-ups, not unlike the crow

or for that matter

the oak

Death is not uncertain

and its advance constitutes

a rude interruption

in the continuing delusion

that *human* is a word

of inestimable value

                Meat

is its real name and other

vibratory levels are not enough

to raise it beyond crow's perch

oak's sunward advance

Prospective uncertain loops back

on itself sinking deeper into its recess

knowing any hour is right for making the contours

worthy of eternity

            No consolation

only endurance

Uncertain advances rudely

penetrate the *dear ones*, leave

them roadside, glimpsed

in rear view mirror

until inevitable bend

in the world

Leaving and coming both agree

renewal's heart evades syntactic

expectations' lines extended threshold

into obscene uncertain topologies

never enough senses infinitely

                            Perfection's

cruelties impose regular *ism* spasms

and Hungarians are no exception

though surviving tanks' advance

down Karepesi út raises clichés

to a level of rage no Utopia

should have to endure

If he swings at you, duck and aim

for his nose with everything

you've got

   Power to the people

is a bit too vague in that regard

unless people contracts to a

singularity of such usefulness

it folds up and fits neatly

into a hidden pocket, leaving

bloody heap on the sidewalk

to find his own socially

significant alignments

     Revolution

is nothing if not a run in with real

hard definitions aching

for a fight while rudely advancing

on uncertain in no terms the sentence

can figure before stopping

[Interlude]

(*for Joanne*)

"You can't out drink the Angel of Death"

—Ed Sanders

Death comes in the night

and in the morning

Death comes for lunch

and tea

[*That he does know takes some shewing.*]

I first met Uncertain at a party

to celebrate the end of the last

nation

    The air that night settled

with the confidence of a banker

hawking sub-prime mortgages outside

an Oklahoma City Sunday School

          Outside in

          this case in

          dicating quiddity deficits

in the spatio-temporal

spectro-fabric, the weave

you dig? here? now? rolling out

the other side of some black

hole machine, some spectral

loom in Leaving's mind

[*How might I be mistaken about my assumption*

that I was never on the moon?]

Uncertain was having none of it. "Realism?"

she said. "Really?" Scorn, a good word

in most sentences, fails to uphold

it's responsibility here leaves

Uncertain uncertain as to the outcome

of this syntactical loggerheads

[The work comes to me, a crystal flood

contains the proposition *the work comes*

and the proposition *me*, pre-positioned in an attitude

of prepositional reception

Me proposes a site of inter

section within the uncertain framework

established on numerous proven errors

recomposed into dependent clauses

left to hang in the breeze at the end

of the sentence — tra-la

                    Traversed by desire

leads to laborious accumulations

of interstitial art eruptions

Then the border

recedes in rear view mirror

and uncertain advances

toward the South China Sea all hot

to duke it out, looking for a little

Set-action spewing darkness

into geo-political pot

of recognizable thumping

              Mantic

initiatory ordeals struggle to find

purchase in a topsy-turvy world

of giddy wrong-way Corrigan

encounters full of *mysterium iniquititas*

outbursts and extreme cruelty

vortices packaged as more

entertainment value for your buck,

all fired up to hang 'em high

and drop kick them through the goal

posts of life, but mistake uncertain

for an easy lay and grab its nether

regions in a sanctioned display

of daddy zeal

> [*Why would it be* unthinkable
> *that I should stay in the saddle*
> *however much the facts bucked?*]

> OK, when stuck
>
> deal with it, when lost
>
> consult the stars, listen
>
> for the ocean
>
> Improper
>
> uncertain advances across moon's
>
> buttery face lead to promiscuous
>
> encounters with mnemonic wreckage
>
> and nostalgia for magnetic north

It doesn't have to fit

but it does have to resist

spinning wheels' dooby

dooby doo and go

*som*ewhere

Heaven and earth

remain expectant, angels want more

attention given previous rescue

operations, an address

to imbricated densities

complicities of seen

and unseen in hierophantic

abracadabra

The beginning word

in the was

so to speak, more

sleight of uncertain syntactical

shuffle's give and take

with the first sight of the mountain

shaved to the ground, donkey

engine roar, trees bounced

over earth's maimed flank

toward a modest ranch

style bungalow in Chula Vista

whose pretty view long ago

went down under the bull

dozer, a tic in someone's economic

indicator, a fluctuation in the GDP

(Grand Democratic Predations)

What does it mean, the hint

of angels asks? Who is at stake?

Be careful—Harvey is watching.

> [I can't be making a mistake—but some day,
>
> rightly or wrongly,
>
> I may think I realize
>
> that I was not competent to judge]

It does go on, letter after letter, word

after word, a book

unwritten being writ

Chapter 4
The pragmatics of to belong as not belonging:
uncertain ontological whims and communal
phantasies

Uncertain leaps ahead, excited for a little

pragmatic whimsy, a bit of onto-folderol

in the name of you could almost say

the Rose if it hadn't been done

to death

      Still, there it is, steel

dust harsh sea wired return through

sympathies and affinities juicy

elaborations

      A juicy world belongs,

initiates action at quantum level

uncertain, rattles the box disturbing

any number of felines whose caterwaul

reverberates with music

of the spheres

      The Jaguar World follows

cats as night follows shadows' ineluctable

modalities—if in fact *to operate magic*

is nothing other than to marry

the world

to belong

is its still, sleek gliding, Harvey

out of the black truck

transformed

        theriomorphic

        eschaton precursor

        Jaguar World

longing rises in flame flickers'

song, to go *with* but without

the cling extension, Jack's CloggD

in the certain light Reilly brought

to Jaguar knowledge

even though *yet to come*

in the ways time toys

with humans, memory

holding nocturnal sun

form to contraction which

expands in ways of animals

come forth in judgment

trees their witness

stones the voice of reason

The load of ganga spreads

light and a handful

of poetry stirs essential

disturbance flows back

and forth over icy Stoli

Pauli Girl, a joint-

talk company of inestimable

valuation in the half price

cosmos of fully guaranteed

solutions to what

ails you recalls the Rose

but supine and bound

to Doom Program's

Dollar Day sub-routine's

erotically re-engineered stuff

into perfectly satisfactory

mass conclusion phantasm

The pragmatics of to belong

begins in desire as matter

of *composition as explanation*

of Blake's four-fold in the shadow

of contraction's Empire

of inches and ells

        To belong

        screams from the bleachers

        red face twisted with hate

        ballpark *mysterium*

        iniquitatus in the guise

        of William Bendix, an untranslatable

        quantum of white being still

        stands for Hephaestus (with a goofy

        smile) in the right light, each

        confined to memory's shadows

        but no less here for all that

        obliteration, a good guy

        anyway, till to belong as belonging

        swells with tumescent

        not us, turns pragmatic

        grabs a rope

Ontological whims enter through talk

turns eschatonic: uncertain incursions

animate dramas wrested

from theo-coitus-interruptus

mental frustration pits, turning

to belong inoperative outside

not to belong as a dynamic

of further always already—

Pass the Stoli

To belong struggles for an image

beyond communion stadia

grotesqueries' twisted shouts

at limping singularity

in the midst

              Love, language

death pull chairs up to the table

raise the stakes with divinatory

gestures invoke the faculty intuits

a movement of descent into matter

of the worthy suitor's claim

to exist and consequent differential

ranges of glow where glow

draped in ivy, intoxicated

> *Lynx-purr, and heathery smell of beasts,*
>
> *where tar smell had been,*
>
> *sniff and pad-foot of beasts*
>
> *eye-glitter out of black air*

To belong as not belonging is a

school yard, first day in the System

hiding behind the piano, lured out

—as clear as if it was tomorrow—

the strange woman beckoning

from motherless space, delivers us

into an outside of swings and sand

and a girl who loves sand so that we

never hear the bell, what does a bell

have to do with a girl and sand

then look up to limp, empty swings

abandoned silence till the strange woman

steps out the door, gathers us

into the world of bells, of to belong

as belonging, the communion

of bells announcing the end

of girls and sand

Other questions

abound in Uncertain's luxurious *contre*

temp with to belong percolates

in not belonging's flicker among time's

hieroglyphs, not as a sign of interim

arrangements, an in the midst of

comparison's leaf in the leaves

but alone with the limp swings

Screaming is useless

It's only a tooth held by a thread

of stubborn flesh you could just wait

but they want it out

and no struggle can stand

against hard hands, squeeze

pry, hold, tie the thread

to massive door, a moment

lost to time's tricks now dances

across the page in letters'

dos a dos with to belong

Screaming is useless

It's only the necessity of inflicting

pain on flesh, its weakness

it's only the necessity of the defeat

of resistance, of not belonging

screams into the circled faces

Screaming is useless

Later they talk of war, compare

flesh's puckered wounds in summer glare

To belong as not belonging

watches, cranks the ice cream maker

as hands hold a small body

down, revelation looms

other hands in other climes

of divorced reason's

ontological whims

In the following section we will examine ontological whims as a symptom of unresolved Oedipal issues compounded by archetypal conflicts with paternal energy and repressed memories of hard hands. All memories will be subject to examination at the door and may be detained and strip searched in the event of reasonable grounds to suspect that the guilty party was knowingly in receipt of contraband articles of faith.

We will also explore therapeutic responses including electrical recalibration of wetware and retuning mnemonic condensers in harmony with standard submission intervals in order to block access to unregulated mental states known to harbour and breed whimsy and whims.

Then there's our home
on Natives' land—O Canada

you are fucked

        As you have fucked others so

you shall stew in the rancid pit

of past sins' suppurating

soul wound oozes toxins into every

trip to Walmart or Holts, every

icing call in every arena (especially

old barns) where oblivious

waits in queue between periods

hoping for a hot dog

before the second period bell

Under the ice

blood soaked earth churns

OK, maybe that's melodramatic

even trite, but to belong as not

belonging doesn't care as long

as the queue is visible

eating itself in auto-cannibalistic

over determination, as long as the lines

at snack bar, checkout stand

shine forth in all their tawdry

finery, Empire's glorious coat

of arms, strip mall ascendant

on a field of fallen forests

decimated people rampant

To belong as not belonging

is to leave leaving

face the music

and dance, an inevitable

series of steps in any household

educated in the way

of Sinatra

Is it hegemony's

recalibrated exercise of expectation's

habits, "common knowledge"

resonates as always

just out of sight

declared To Belong at the last

G20, or was it the G7, or maybe

that Appalachian bunch

sent the war machine PR

into overdrive but stripped to belong

as not belonging to any prospects

beyond nostalgia's

through-the-roof-beauty

shots, each decapitated phrase

framed by a new golly

in crippled memory's sudden

miraculous cure

                    Dance, anyway

survives the disaster in other

devices, sitting down, standing

up or just metonymically

hoofing across the page

in defiance of discourse's

demand for an end to investigation

of each move inevitably leads

down into the darkest regions

of depraved whimsy

cha cha cha

    The promise of pragmatics lingers

    swerves the prosodic instant

    toward indelicate considerations

    of four four's patriotic flatus

    as a symptom of ontological dementia

        Half the fun

        is getting there

            The door swings out

            & Jaguar World emerges, soft

            throaty purr caresses shadow's

            uncertain boundaries—if it's

            the sound of death, purr

            back, stroke shadow, leave

vanquishing to the sadly

enlightened

To belong as not belonging

knows excommunication looms

within familiar clutch of hard

hands

      Held down, forced, over

whelmed, language rips

world from earth's flesh

leaves enlightened stretches

of wounded flank exposed

majesty's twisted wreckage

a matter of fact where matter's

lost mother mourns for her child

fallen into the ways

of hegemony's dismissal leaves

outside to stories' smoke

and mirror slide into silence

Poof

Who's yer Daddy?

A menagerie of signs sheaths

familiar view, the Bay evades

stretches but gets tagged

by *extends,* a sign of resistance

or maybe just aversion

to elastic metaphors

                Still, there it is

(n't), depth's clarity as far

as the eye can sustain

embryonic potency in the light

of another day outside

the conquest of every little

glimmer of what can't

be sold, I want I want

belonging to hard hands'

certainty

To let eyes wander over fanciful

objects opens discourse of roots

to flutter as a state of to belong

as not belonging

No arbitrary

echoic flim-flam contempt

in whimsy's caprice, just shiver

vision's disturbance of daily

goat frisk, a mindful caper through

boulevards and alleys

in 1899

> That's history for you

> before the System claimed

> its story from another clime

> hung it out to dry

> in all that light of conclusion's

> ends

> And still the Rose flutters

> outside the birdhouse hole, beak

> full of fresh meat for the hunger

> inside, outside sways

> to wind's whim, signals flutter

> full of fresh configurations

> of light filtered through green

> screen's telegraphic dance

> To belong as not belonging

sings with it, a little off key

from the harmony of the spheres

but charming in its innocent

suspension of regulatory

harmonics in the face

of the *tremendum*

                Errant music

ensues, belongs as not belonging

caught up in frisky caprices

the Bay's surge bringing incursions

of *mysterium conjunctionis*

Bruno named love

                Anything goes

            against hard hands'

              clutch of music's

                errant throat

Taxonomies of uncertain

and uncertain taxonomies open

with revolt, demands

for immediate recognition

of stone's pov in relation

to new energy vectors'

solar quickening vibration lingo

    The sub-sub librarian

    would no doubt have a thing

    or two to add to that

    but remains bifurcated

    in the vaults which sometimes

    disguise warrens

        Initially taxonomies

seem the way to go—folio

octavo, duodecimo ring with genuine

literary irony for those in the know

may even deserve inclusion

in the Anthology of Best

Intergalactic Taxonomies

                            No taxonomy

without representation, however,

calls into question *wind water*

shift rise surge entangled

chaos with sure fire belonging rituals'

potent display of US metaphysics

apocalyptic precursor

twitter effluvia—give me

liberty or give me a hefty

line of credit so I can buy

a Walmart air con—what

climate change?—Bomb

the Chinks but don't tread

on my knock off Versace

make America great

again camo tee-shirt

(3 bucks what

a steal)

Beginning with vegetable

uncertain or animal uncertain

won't explain light's

strange liquidity leaves nominal

arrangements illuminated pulse

surging toward shore

when the wind shifts

to the north east

        Taxonomy watches it

        crash against rocks

        while trying to distinguish

        sexual desire, sexual love

        and erotic play in pursuit

        of a more perfect union

        as spider arranges husks

        of its hunger along web's

        radial spread traps

        entangled light too

1) Socio-economic disparities determined by inequities of race, gender, and class causes
2) Incursions of eternal *eventforms* causes
3) Shit happens causes
4) Your mama causes
5) Just because causes
6) Sub-atomic quantum effect weird causes
7) Random non-cause causes
8) Sex causes
9) Evil causes
10) Uncertain causes

Lunch with Uncertain in Deleuze's Diner

Anexact essences magical knowledge

crystallizes time's nonhuman becoming

births individuating world's

multiplicity of discontinuous

durations anorganic distilled

cosmic blocs intense vibrational

states of matter in unforeseen

dimensions of sound, colour

and time mapped singular points

intensive feeds irreducible

spread of entangled processes'

nomadic, anarchic distribution

modes where diagrams of immanence

in creative zone of indiscernibility

and real virtual potencies breeds

a sure fire maelstrom of meaning,

conjectural images, and an infinite

network of energetic relays

exchanges, transitions, affective

vertigo in the face of imbricated

ambulant couplings open

a delicate sieve through which

a little pure chaos

may enter

A Taxonomy of Uncertain

1) Sort of uncertain
2) Moderately uncertain
3) Stumped uncertain
4) Skeptical uncertain
5) On the verge of affective vertigo in the face of imbricated ambulant couplings uncertain
6) Bewildered uncertain
7) Flummoxed uncertain
8) Sunk in a maelstrom of meaning uncertain
9) Beyond the pale from a great height uncertain
10) On the horns of a dilemma uncertain
11) Stopping by woods on a snowy evening pretending you're uncertain uncertain
12) Ludwig Wittgenstein uncertain

Follow the blue line leads

to more perplexity than a line

deserves as often occurs

with unruly taxonomies in heat

during an era of homeopathic

doses of Apocalypse

The line

leads into the Warren, rich

with *contained*, war vibe's vicious

enclosure, compulsory

Killer-Unit Processing Centre

promises to turn your boy

into a monster in no time flat

                              Cluster comes later

with city's crammed space

proliferate passage's

confused knots of purpose

                        Follow

the yellow line differs

superficially but telic

considerations being

what they are leads

to the same Door

                        Follow the red line

                        ditto

Lines of men and lines

on the floor—red, blue

yellow, green—a difficult

intricate knot dance into machine's

maw, a neat bit of alliteration

meant to become a turning

an intention of *m,* closed mouth

agent of the speechless *mysterium*

mmmmm, mmmmm

     Taxonomies of mystery fail

     to initialize in the light of uncertain

     antecedents leave *cause*

     in a state of unknown origin

     Then what?

The bus pulls up outside

the Warren, each store front

feeds gathered bodies into lines

that stop start stop down branching

halls, lines of men follow lines

on the floor

        then the acid hits

big time, can opener moment

cosmic death horror spilling

from the burst continuum

machine's infernal roots

each unfolding moment

into red face man's demonic

scream

GET BACK

RETURN TO THE LINE

GET BACK IN LINE

                              but that can't happen

since by this time

a number of other dimensions

have joined the party

                              (which is the time

of mystery's obfuscation

shrunken apprehension

regularized cruelties arrayed electric

specificity of contorted

cavernous mouths)

When taxonomical wreck staggers

from the line, force kicks in, hard hands

drag it down coloured lines

station to station, passage

after passage, red line, yellow line

green line, blue line

till approved Killer-Unit Status

Ready for Training stamped and fed out

Doom Program Door

egress or is it ingress, coloured

lines leading beneath mind's

mountains of Mordor, red

face SCREAMS and SCREAMS

of shame till taxonomical wreck

snaps

     leaps up

          screams into the red face

screams out of line, screams

into the scream

and then sudden ejection

into sun baked street

a dazed speck blinking

in blistered city's maze

Deep warrens and wide

beneath Mordor Mountains'

uncertain geography, locale

to be determined

A Taxonomy of Warrens

1) Walled City of Kowloon warren
2) if I can just get offa this LA freeway (© Jerry Jeff Walker) warren
3) rat's nest warren
4) under the Mountains of Mordor warren
5) rabbit's warren warren
6) metaphoric Unconscious warren
7) Warren Tallman warren
8) Kenneth Warren warren
9) garden of forking paths warren
10) how the fuck did I end up here warren (see also Taxonomy of Uncertain #7)
11) a veritable warren of misconceptions warren
12) compulsory Killer-Unit Processing Centre warren

Scattering a few aleatory

remarks on the ground

is a good way to start

if you can find the ground

Divining helps in the right

light and may illuminate

imperceptible forces project

themselves into vocabulary

known to have followed the blue

line, not to mention the red

threads through the Warren

abandoned polite taxonomies

in full dress uniform

screaming get back in line

NOTE: Leaving the line—whatever its colour—has been known to give rise to aberrant taxonomies of discontent whose *in the light of* leaves hopeless confusion devised tactics suitable to violate syntactic relationship to the world and initiate adventures of sense in the midst of burning forests, weather phenomena previously thought to exist only in certain quadrants of Jupiter's larger moons, and random collective and individual acts of misery and mass murder in the name of God, leaving bodies to be disposed of, to drift away in columns of *honourable* smoke.

Grand Mother's *housemind* is figured

pointless, arrested in secret

passage through walls beneath draped

vestiges from before the war

Saturday morning noir, old

lady smell, powder, corsets, angel

food, Deco street lamps spilled

shadow into boulevards'

crumbling glamour recalled

in light's shimmer on submerged

stones left by glacial retreat

                              A *storm cellar*

in a land of no storms, insistent

mark of leaving, having left

without leaving, boxes stacked

in recesses of dank earth

filled with ice skates

in the desert, The Phantom

a railroad, father mysteries

from before the war

A Taxonomy of War

1) World War wars
2) Mental Combat wars
3) Wars to End All Wars wars
4) War on Christmas wars
5) Asymmetrical War wars
6) Ongoing operations to eliminate all pockets of resistance wars
7) Poetry War (©Tom Clark) wars
8) All Out War wars
9) Peacekeeping wars
10) Outside the door at the end of the coloured lines wars

Each room's potent

passage, spatial adventure

crawling out closet window

into mystery's chiaroscuro game

love and death in tough

story's choreographed embrace

with the architecture

of a flickering world

      Then another shooting drops

      into the field, an interruption

      approaches daily regularity as war

      seeps through tissue of interdimensional

      discriminations sewing confusion

      in systemic despotisms as it

      mows down music lovers

      paroxysm of sheer life hatred

      leaks from some zone of unmitigated

      pain at the point

      of maximum contraction

Follow the blue line into taxonomy's

death driven discernment

of utility to the Machine, sorting

flesh's agility following the blue

line, yellow line, without compunction

yields to despotism of signs scream

stay in line or face the rage

of the screaming red face

> The old woman in black lurks
>
> in the margins, patient, waits
>
> for the noise to stop, recalls
>
> a taxonomy of roses dances
>
> with the light, catches it
>
> in shifting patterns flow with the flow
>
> of earth and sky through her
>
> fingers
>
>> Bodies flow through salvaged
>>
>> beds, onions, trunks, jewelry glitter
>>
>> chiles, knives, jicama, coins
>>
>> to the eternal beat of Mel's
>>
>> Slick Stick One Man Band
>>
>> in *wantneed's* itinerant
>>
>> distribution links

The old woman in black stands

at the pile of chiles, sorting

is a fine sieve, a syntactic net

in found place among powder,

corsets, vestiges of before the war

tucked into subterranean nook

in the storm cellar where roots

dangle without irony

from earthen walls

She must have been waiting

all those years

for her text

suddenly become a map

A Taxonomy of Texts

1) Interlinear to texts texts
2) University text book texts
3) People in the rear view mirror texts
4) Freudian dream text texts
5) Contextual texts
6) Anti-textual non-text texts
7) Essential texts
8) Shamanic vocalic incantatory texts
9) Itinerate disposition of wild signs texts
10) An old woman dressed in black sorting chiles text

Her hands too fast to follow,

taxonomies of touch past light's speed

in crowd surge, sweat, coconut

scented sun block, beer

Mel's Slick Stick rendition

of the music of the spheres

to keep Time, her blurred hands

knowing beyond theurgy's pale

and idolatries of history, impossible

intimacy with unimaginable

animal dwells deep in the thought

of the Rose and artisanal taxonomies

of creative destruction, destructive

creation, her hands a blur

gnostic flesh sorting

    If you say tomato, and I say tomahto

    are taxonomic virtualities invoked

    beyond the usual kind, or is the difference

    merely a fluke of unconditional

    levity looking for a way to evade

    untoward advances of serious

    literary ambition

Who's yer Daddy

reverberates beyond immediate

textual locale in prize winning

attention to permission's

dubious welcome

                    while uncertain outcomes

wake in derelict neighbourhoods

where gangs of taxonomical atavisms

chant names of mystery entities

in kaleidoscopic order

Chapter Six
Interlinear to some simplified examples of chaos

The initial problem lacks room

between lines to stretch chaos

beyond daily deformations

and simple political developments

spilling from unnamed zone

of directional disintegration

Left is right and right has gone

over the edge where chaos

programs the restoration

of the Brazen Bull and Iron

Maiden Economic Program

all dolled up as great

again lollapalooza

torch lit parade of colour

challenged button down rhythm

less morons marching

to their inner Sousa stomp

                    Left is right

leaves interlinear stranded

in cavernous hall attempting

to explain Jacobin realities

and 1789 French National

Assembly spatial divisions to a crowd

of Puritans demand immediate

access to the Horde and inclusion

in the 2020 Anthology of Best American

Selves guaranteed to be nice

and with prepackaged context modules

designed to replace the stress of thinking

with authorized moral knowledge

          Incomprehensible lurks between

          interlinear to all matter

          of answers stretched out

          and arrived in arrays

          of red, green, yellow,

          and blue resolutions

                    Hands at its heart

          twist knots out of

          phantom clutch, squeeze

digestible portions brewed

from codes prefigured in workshops

of immaculate possession

       Meanwhile, some simplified examples of chaos

       head to Florida trailing clouds of dough

       and talking of Michaelangelo's

       current market value

              while the sea

              kisses tee

       off markers leaves sodden

       ball to bob away on waves

       of unregulated archonic hunger

       fuels Doom Program's

       Clearcut Aesthetic

       interlinear to children

       quietly bleed

       in bombed out remains

       of various agreements

Broken threads' frayed remains

spin a compass

needle confronted by theory

of the subject in a dark alley

as a way out through lines

extend into every woody stretch

toward light's seduction

incorporated in winter

sky lace revelations

                    Interlinear

murmurs breach trans

opalescent glow between

instances spread

through neuronic delusions

in animate disturbance of laminar

cohesion leaves ruined wake

to go to the dogs, an archaic

wreck of more human

age inequities uncompromised

isolate phantasm

                    Blood lines

narrate interstitial coupling

fiction's grip on crippled

imaginations of pure conundrums

mongrel real

                Extensive lineation

stretches into cerulean mirage

a vast beyond demands

a good topic sentence to hold

it to line of thought growls

into dark outside strange doors

insistent mystery

                Dawn speaks

context, another moment

exposed break calls eyes

to cracked sky names leave

relics of our passage

to stutter of rising

water, perpetual black plastic

package after package, carefully wrapped

banana peels, coffee grounds,

snot crusted tissues and meat

rotting on the bone

dumped and buried

in savage-seized land

Word mystery exceeds line's

measured tones and rocky

sense, pierced by unsubstantiated

but substantial flights into images

of sky entangled temporal

dislocations lost to excessive

neon misprision's blinding

allegorical occupation

and border interrogation

> The line marks history's family
>
> expulsion parlayed into umbilical
>
> distinctions of war's acceptable
>
> extension beyond disestablishment
>
> and authorized slaughter
>
> of pre-existing "condition's"
>
> animal threat to dominion,
>
> and taxes, of course, bedevil
>
> the wilderness with unacceptable
>
> demands to share, a being
>
> modality beyond pale
>
> faced trans-Atlantic cupidity
>
> leavened with regicidal ravening

                    clear cut soul wreckage

                    leaks between lines

                    scroll down screen naming

                                          fate patsy

Interlinear is a large wet tongue, a cooling device

of immense intelligence and capacity

for interspecies admixtured spit

swapping

    Laminar traffic flow indicates smooth

    sailing all the way home where home

    expects to be found in positions of unusual

    familiarity

        Having set sail, cruise control demands

        some kind of accounting, blends into formulas

        of contempt forged out of alloyed doubts

        by a thread barely holds the imminent encounter

        rock offers

            Hunger manufactured in factories of Really Cheap

            Stuff battles with dissonant anthems interlinear

            to proclamations and declarations of the usual

            deceit

The Deceiver, well known in former neighbourhoods

lost to Developers' Blade, promises to come

in on budget

    Interlinear risked collision with established flow delivers
    a load of lineation—think twitterless,

    no clinamen, no—who cares, such fun

    in shattered calm, pleasures roiling

        Simplified

        examples of chaos may result

        in disrobing

        reactions in populations

        determined by

        aggregate wealth

        division into I

        want it all

        motherfucker go

        back where you

        came from

The tongue announces affection across the Great Divide instills
terror's untroubled bloody tooth and claw chaos taxonomies of
order in minds of girdled girth

Then spread mind's embodied receiver tastes nature and logos
in the afterglow thinking with Whitehead brings to shepherd's
life, what animals have to teach us about politics, a veritable
library of combinatory feral asystemic forays into joyous blends
of random stacks' titular uncertain together

Interlinear to *uncertain rain forests refuse to populate* and
adumbrations of their exemplary syntax lies a world of
Umwelten vibratory field proliferation *chori* wail in exquisite
dis-harmonies of hunger fear shared food puzzles solved wet
tongues' breeched boundaries strange unpredictable rescues
necessities of considered death and pain *withfor* others' pain
joy *forwith* others' joy reeling through chaotic syntactic
imbrications entangled asymbolic corporeal tendencies surpass
the given water seeking bum sniffing sensorium in vagaries of
vocalic exuberance

Gods weep in the margins suggests excludes as 800 strokes
a minute machine roar induced ear-ring swallows memory's
lines of flight, oily universal joint chugging along, cacophonous
harmonies of aural assault and concatenation tending toward
illusions of working class hero manufactured in factories of
inimitable identity's smoke and mirror interlinear transitions
till it snaps

Errant stars burn in love-of-knowledge-

of-love forms, reforms, uniformed

figures of the border

loom out of Detroit night

                Rusted blue flapping

angel-winged Nova hits the road

into inimitable distance as explanations

fail in I-know-not-what encounters

with mind's landscapes preserved

in perfect mystery of divinatory

mania's resplendent flavour

                Lines flicker

down invisible screen

fate's unfolding list

zero/one, yes/no, jail/

the road's hallucinatory

distance, snake-eyes/seven

come eleven

release and into primeval

night of America's

blood-lust dream's brutal manifest

rest-stop punctuated

      return

to interrupted love-ruins

trailing clouds of broken salvation

justice fuelled phantasmagoria's

perfectly arranged redemption

         Spell it S-P-A-C-E

or T-E-R-R-O-R, settled habits

of its conquest (they always speak

of *conquest*, even of Spicer's

sister Death) transformed into grids

immense asphalt scars

gouged across its flank

where parables of success circulate

through bone heaps invisible domain

judged by the moon, sentenced

by stellar disinterest, punished

with a terrible silence fills the world

with *musick, musick, musick*

and thud of plastic bags of left

over food, non-functioning essential

appliances, torn clothing, and countless

Styrofoam trays stained

with blood and engineered

to withstand eternity's

patient work

On the other side

home's mythy hills golden-humped

dreamscape spreads out

in pornographic splendour

as Angel-winged Nova descends

flapping out of cannibal mountains

scarred by interlinear exuberance

ears ringing with machine roar

carnal destruction

while Kingdom's

proximity knowledge pulses

close at hand, another manifest

of indifferent words

Where

you have to go requires uncertain

to raise the letter beyond

logical outcome in no further

sense than *the golden hills*

of home's form as it percolates

through rain forests and pre-Cambrian

Shield, breeds metaphysical dis

content in regions of nostalgia's

pain in the heart

You can go home again

but when you get there

watch out for the thought of arrival

leaves you naked in someone's bed

waiting for them to come

from another room

who will never arrive

Then you are home

wherever the sentence has led

interlinear to simplified examples

of on your own continue to sit

silently beyond the threshold

announces new dispensation

of home's uncertain with

held body

Once arrived home, obvious imperatives become several:

When hitting the road, use gloves, and never forget the vanishing point is an old fighter's art trick;

Remember, work is not essential—although eating is beneficial;

Interlinear instances of "life's ironies" should be embraced on the front seat, tongue deeply inserted in a once in a lifetime spit swapping, tonsil massaging erotic extravaganza;

Iterations of chaos when it did then not fine detritus come will occasions and spurts;

Allow the sentence free rein in continued unauthorized smooches as an antidote to linear inclusion;

Abandoned in a naked bed, embrace home as an uncertain outcome.

softfleshtornfleshswollenfleshmoistfleshburnt-
fleshtinglingfleshemaciatedfleshdecomposing-
fleshembryonicfleshpulsatingfleshcontracted-
fleshsaggingfleshfirmfleshbleedingfleshsmelly-
fleshdarkfleshpinkishfleshscarredfleshsmooth-
flesherectfleshswollenfleshtuckeredfleshpuck-
eredfleshhunkeredfleshstellarflesh

Harvey pops in from between lines' endeavours, having
disappeared some poems ago. Never sure of his place in
the poem's geography but never able to escape its lure—not
to mention the pull of its sentence—he recollects Jaguar's
World's lost kingdom of elemental fleshing at the Dog Park
where puppy roils exceed, race, and tumble through ex-
changes of above and below, in and out, before and behind
leaves Shalt and Shaltnot to argue on the sidelines out past
the abandoned tennis court

Ah, man, he says, don't forget to watch for signs the
tremendum leaves around the dog park, don't forget histo-
ry rhymes with mystery, and the Big Yam (a mythological
force emerged from beyond the Chaosphere to conquer
Twitter) is an angel of annunciation, a sign of Time's Fore-
play with emergent world beyond our ken

With Deleuze at the Dog Park

non-conventional entities excessive

in-between blazed path's

emergent variations processual

zone of indiscernibility

between *is* and *couldbe*

self-surpasses imperatives

of immanence in ludic excess

and frivolous expenditure's

processual primacy leaves

normative ethics supernormalizing

movement of vital inventiveness'

catalytic subjectivity

without a subject

        woof

Interlinear to internal and external

leaks a world of difference at verge,

inexternal folds of night

beyond Detroit for instance

Spaces unfold *fleshmind's*

compositional hoot

motherfather matrix paternal

scission opens into Dad's

death mewl, the pain

of all Father's whose child stands witness

to their last drunken wallow

in manifest destiny's subdivision

of the soul into lots

of unquenchable hunger

for a new Olds

        Textual obligations require shifts

        of foothold not to mention

        a strong stomach for unexpected turns

        into precipitous paths along crumbled

        plunge through modal intensities

                    Dead

        father announces symbolic

        importance with requisite

        fanfare but only if you lose

        sight of who he is

                                    Was

                                            Thennow

                Amen

                                    Some relief

                                    Getting a gig

                                    in Madrid's no

                                    sweat for kid

                                    from Fresno

                                    do wop sha do

We run the fun
The Boss says, *cease & desist*
your frivolous italics

Interlinear roads wend
familiar ground intend
ease of passage

Outside line's forbidden

control scrawl sprawls

wantonly

Wall's tobacco soaked stink

and drink's unquenchable come

hither pool redly

If the potential to walk the dog

is the potential to not walk the dog

who's walking the dog?

Interlinear to begin

& end lurches through

folds of night beyond Detroit

      Each choice names

      a new world and chaos

      lurks in its interlinear

      excesses, its adamantine

      encounter with hidden

      roadside entrance erupts

      into textosphere from other

book fatally compromises

delusions of intact voice

as justification for authentic

doggerel

      Conversation does not

compare though the two

do draw other apples

—honey crisp whose name

is worth two bucks a kilo—

and oranges into integrity

busting exchange of textual

fluids mingling quiddities

in pornographic reconfigurations

full frontal diction action

money shot in lawless

margins beyond the pale

self's meagre image store

"between"   "among"

Robin wrote, convivial

carnival home's insistent

going forth into another

choice, an other world

of apples and oranges

orapples and appanges

furious carnamorous affair

of ingestion, world's flesh

opening to further curve of its

inward enunciation, tongue

hard against each consonant

fact, carneous grace, each

esculent vowel cupped gently

in the tongue's bowl of primitive resistance

to run-time dogma's obligatory

clarities

Interlinear to unitas

states lurks a field

of exorbitant push if

you don't lose your nerve

when the road disappears

Interlinear to raptor and rapture

implicates a sharp point

of engagement with *mysterium*

of the tremendum's come

hither oracular eruption

Interlinear to Father Knows

Best and Donna Reed reeks

of early times desperation

for a touch left numb

by brutal violation

      America, we salute you

      who are about to choke

      on the smoke

      of your dream

            Charred black flesh dangles

      interlinear to when in the course

      of human events

      another noose

Interlinear to simplified

examples of chaos disappears

in the night outside

Detroit headed west

looking for geographies imagination

fed the exiled heart

Chapter Seven
A Methodology for Verifying Fugitive
Apparitions in Uncertain Glances

Sense is overrated in theatres of uncertain

glances modulate states of vibratory

tuning often left to their own devices

or lost in shuffle fugitive apparitions

thrive in

      Harvey for instance

haunting the edge of the poem

inquisitor, provocateur

to the angels who hang around

the corner outside jazz clubs in Cleveland

                              Music

informs the wind of its meaning

drifts into a poem a hundred years

later, well beyond expiry

date, a veritable fairy tale

prince whose kiss shouts Arise

                    Harvey

mounts his bike and rides, bound

for uncertainty, bound for the magic

recognition yields poppies

flowering in stony detritus left

by the last Ice, more than a mile

high just here where it stopped

and the world emerged

in looming cold truth

                  You *can*

make this shit up and when you do

be prepared to enter

its consequences, the rest of the poem

waiting on the next page, taut

with excitement, waiting to see

if these unfolding words

will stretch into a story

worthy of the end that came

before it reeling toward

a civilized smooch

                  Blame the aurochs

                  they didn't resist hard enough, didn't

                  fight the pen, cut off from the indifferent

                  range of their hunger

                  by sticks or dogs or wire, didn't

                  trample the assholes rounding them up

calling them *doggies* in Sumerian

didn't make for their further *home*

before the song overtook their range

and the whole lurid affair followed—

bombs, bullets, every weaponized

advance, every advance weaponized

beyond pitiful delusions' pale

of a new better light bulb, a new

better car—this one drives itself

occasionally takes out some random

 meat in the middle of the street—

another flavoured deodorant

for your crotch eliminates repellant

flesh's last lingering animal

stink of fugitive apparitions

in the shadow of the Ice

imagines it all laid out

in a catalog of exquisite

labels or glass cabinets in little

square rooms, even the poems

captured, alphabetized, stored

in a great poem warehouse—resistance

is futile, present yourself

to be penned

An Idyll

When mom is drunk and full of sand

She laughs and sings, grabs your hand

Happily bounces from wall to wall

Lurches, stumbles down the Hall

Mythically falls through an open door

Screams and cries, writhes on the floor

The swaying now a sinful site

Of lame transgression's limping blight,

Daddy's claim to prior right

Of dark recess

Some caves were meant for pirate stash

And others for a secret bash

Where diversions dance with funny twists

Grin in the dark from foetid mists'

Cinematic blur. Others hold

Secrets only serpents know

Slithering down toward earth's hot core

Through roots and stones and bones galore

Mouldering remains from some dim shore

Receding

Anagogic blows descend on fallen

Hope for joyous union all in

One big happy family,

But all that darkness now set free

Stumbles on toward Hall's conclusion

Woven through each deep contusion

Glancing smacks, relentless flurry

Rain on innocence with fury

Jealous gods bequeath to bury

Illicit knowledge

Nothing more now can to be said

Of Dad and Mom and the Dancing Lad

Who fell through the door in the Hall's

Receding light into mythy calls

Beyond the blows and imprecations

Hurled on untoward implications

Of forbidden union's wild infection

Rages through each further reflection

Of form's prodigious wild successions

Of love

Mercurial ain't

the half of it, fugitive

apparitions constituting

foundational state of retort

slide into unexpected

bump as eternal grace

strides by on long, taut legs,

spreads a blanket in the shade

down near the lake

surrounded by willows

                  She enters

a figure Uncertain glances in the distance

as the Kykean at Eleusis shows up

along with the dog and fungal

intoxicants' enlarged depth

of field, a processional giving

leads to the unspeakable girl

hooking up with Uncertain, getting

it on in incursions leave current

aggressions against soul and spirit framed

in parental myths kinky event

                                        Fugitive apparition flies

in the face of psychology's Rx

resolutions and literary ambitions,

there's just no explaining it

in terms suitable for Good

Housekeeping's seal of approval

or other canonical manuals of Certain

            The amplified sensorium

            yields vistas of immaculate

            oddity—audacious ain't the half

            of it, a clichéd phrase of repeated

            occurrence and Zenonian

            expectation precipitates further

            vocabulary's excessive deception

            and failure to close in on tortoise

            mock soup and heroic

            conclusions' common terror

            at the thought of *freed, Arise*

            or even a little clarity in the midst

            of jammed up traffic nightmare's

            esoteric revelation in stalled

            sea of red lights as the radio calmly

dissects The Weed's ancient gift

pinned and poked

alphabet of dead letters, T, C, B,

H, D, arrayed in orders of fear

and commodity futures, debated

by doctors, politicians, cops

shrinks and any random agent

of the Doom Program who wants

to leap in and pronounce on

the brain chemistry of 14 year olds

exposed to ecstasies, epiphanies

and just plain old dislocation

into realms of wonder, wandering

unmoored mind adrift in modalities

of the visible fugitive apparitions

like to dawdle in

A fugitive apparition on a speeding motorcycle

breeds a small riot in mnemonic harbours

of proletarian transit, disrupts chatter

precedes entrance into labour's loveless

rearrangement of Stuff's flow, closely chased

by flashing red Doom lights, disappears

into the maze enormous trailers cast

in uncertain night

Restaging ancient pieces of the cult

exits the System, but it's best to keep

in mind profligate gestures

in the mode of Lotte Lenya

as antidote to heartless mind's *expulsion*

in the name of tomorrow's perfect

grace and popular terrains

of terminal satiety

The movement erupts from *Let's Go*

onset of *heartmind*'s vigorous laugh

crosses the street *en masse*

surges into anonymous dark, folds

fugitive apparition into the next

Whiskey Bar's dark arms, whisks

him out of System's clutch

even as lights and sirens converge

out of the dark to put down

 threat of The Small Riot

occupy the night with their howl

then rage through stacked canyons

of desire's boxed fulfillment

cornering, questioning, demanding

surrender, a methodology of terror

meant to stamp uncertain outcome

into a bloody pulp in order's

sacred name and interject fugitive

apparition with certain unmistakable

constraints forged out of that old

familiar stuff, adamantine appeal

into hungers' ever renewed pause

that refreshes

Fugitive apparitions evade linear

designations of directional flow

find themselves in strange places

lurk in the folds of Bake's Oedipal

apparitions ought

to twist and turn

instead of shouting

Arise!

But it did and Red

is the East, too, toward a better world

in birth, hammers going whence the sickles

to play catch up, fugitive from a war

waged on people defending their homes

from those weak of heart, susceptible

to alien abduction
                          Fugitive has the ring

of an ancestor flying, a condition

of howdy to I-prefer-not-to

but requires a methodology beyond

current poetics' enclosures' limited

repertoire, archery at the dark

of the Moon before advanced

technocrats sand-bagged words, stacked

them against the *tremendum's*

mysterium and Uncertain's insistence

on stumble as a basic unit

of cosmological fancy
                          Radium, for instance,

though that didn't turn out

so well for us, did it?

or does stumble require

a different frame of literary reference

say, rhymes with humble, a possible

fumble connected beyond humble

since it's closer to S in some scheme

of things, the T does it, catching

your toe as you pass by fugitive

apparitions and fugitive glances

recapitulate ontogeny

in ways no one suspected

Whose glances bounce off fugitive

determination to escape clutches

such a sentence leads to

with interrogative declarations

of *je ne sais quoi*

        Children ripped

with certainty from mothers'

arms, fathers' arms is no fugitive

apparition, hence the certainty

of its utility to regimes of hatred

a vibrational state emanating

from interdimensional locales known

to harbour regions of inexplicable *dark*

breeds *strict's* containments

in constricting restricted strictures terrify

things that grow, forced to flee as they can,

other terrestrial suggestions

follow in disorderly array,

ripped from the arms

is what it does, ruling

the lowest archon in fits of pique par

for the course Ishmael would say, another

facet of the diamond, flawed

but integral

        To what?

Uncertain asks, uncertain, to which

Methodology offers a scintillant

whirlwind of repartee

commencing with

Up yours

A recent analysis of the evidence suggests that Fugitive Apparitions have been using social media to sow states of uncertainty among ontological a priories in order to disrupt output of congestive narrative failure to exceed. Who is in the story and surprises the teller leaves vertigo to rule syntactic adumbrations with wanton abandon and unpredictable displays of morning's splashes of sunlight illumine fluttering green face of another new world. Appealing to the lucidity of glass-off moments' deep revelations of stones waver beneath rippled assurance of continued passage, Apparitions insist on speaking of minds' their as an indication aliens among us is ourselves though not to rule out uncertain strangers visible only through sideways glances at the dinner table as a sign of supplementary extent. Experts await further studies but have publicly stated that facts are beside the point in this instance. Other instances, too. Chaos is its own anodyne. Other analyses concur.

[The angel, she said,

coming to meet you

on the bridge, do you know

its name?]

                                   Angels

return, dance around the edge, twice

in a day, quiet rhetorical surprises recall

the fall, protective hands, mercy

for a mortal plummet's failed ascent

to their song

                    Earth is no cushion

and there's no escape

from its hard embrace, *Listen,*

sweetie, they sing, but keep

your feet tapping the ground

and never ever try to illuminate

The Human Condition, stick

to the pebbles stretch out

before your new immobile eyes

ineluctable

          terrain of the fallen

                              [This far into strange territory (terrain)

                              and it refuses to cough up place names

                              or even one familiar horizon, wracking

the bush for a glimpse of sky, a rent

and glint of distant water beyond tangled

wall of incessant *thrive*

whose old clutch dwells in weave's

web, wall of each perfect leaf

alive with phantasms and eidolons

of a past, of a whatever happened

to that blue and white '57 Chev

rag top she named Gypsy

sign of *wilder, further* within an order

of compulsory Olds 98s

meaning let's just go see what's up there

where mud track and bush meld

or bush devours it depending on

inclination which drops down and ends

up at the Slough of Despond's

baby brother

Harvey is no help

here where angels

disguise themselves

as fairies, flicker

among the birch

at night, this far

in and still uncertain

terms shimmer in peach

blush on still water's

immense sky, the same

one *inside* where other

shimmer swells

in love

Perfection's apparition beyond the current

jumble of stone's laden with edge shattered

reminder of mile high Ice

flees with Shelley's ghosts before time's

stiff breeze, holding its cap with one hand

"The Internationale" clutched in the other

Meanwhile, prisoners of starvation

still starve, some

also get burned alive

in shoddy factories and

or crushed by a falling roof

the information, if judged *gross*

by Perfection's recent iteration

as Be Nice to Each Other, Or

Else, will get qualified and quarantined

in triggerless Containment Centres

designed to mute equanimity disruptions

and unpleasant goads to thinking

Perfectly safe, a kind of barricade

misses out on Arise's unavoidable

street fight, as well as numerous feelings

induced by *bad* and *uncomfortable*,

though nowhere near as bad as the roof

coming down on you

Perfection's apparition flees down a hall

stumbles, falls into a blind alley

dumpster stink, flash of moon

light on smashed glass shards

little stars in the waste

where empty boxes spill out shadow

Arise

Perfection orders, and Starvation

rides in on a train from Berlin to haunt

central precincts of Perfection's

instrumental hope, heartless

mind's delusional control

written in cracked bones' hieroglyphics

ephemeral music

of tortured screams

agony of petrified mind

    Uncertain's glances fall hopefully

    on The Small Riot erupted, they say,

    from Al-Andalus via The Last

    Whiskey Bar (threatening

    to become a symbol and ruin

the fun) but uninterested

in perfection and glimpsing

it there, packs up its Manifesto

collection (including a rare item dated

Paris 1871 stained according to authoritative

Market analysts with documented

human blood) mementos of other

sojourns, large and small, said to be worth

a small fortune and much sought after

by wealthy collectors and respectable

art prisons

    and retreats to the lunch room

        for a toke

If fugitive apparitions could stumble

down the Hall and fall through the door

they would wake up in an allegory

where more and more meaning poured

out forms of deviant girth and perverse

expectations calibrated to maintain Sphinx

Terror at maximum output levels

to dissuade entrance to the Chamber

at the end of the hall where She now waits

the Unspeakable Girl

                who

despite building anticipation

of forbidden carnal titillation, just wants

to cuddle, talk of methodology, and inquire

as to the rationale for attacking *Coney*

Cunt, sacred site of creation's mysteries,

with laser beams in order to turn

incarnated splendour, majesty, profundity

into "a little beautiful peach"

Are you guys for real

she asks

    This far in and the end rears up

    right in the centre of terra

    incognita, nameless moment

    of maybe understanding

    on the lam, another fugitive

    apparition in the moonlight

    Tempus fugit is a thing people say

    when they think they woke up

Chapter 8
Gluten free pornography,
myth, and your health

Levity is no excuse to take

liberties with belly fat, especially

when naked or otherwise exposed

to Uncertain's often cruel

gaze, and your health, too

a mug's game if you ask

me [a verbal gesture meant to instill

an intimate connection, a familiar

turn of phrase referencing

the idea of Person unafraid

of gluten]

      Levitation, on the other

hand remains contentious in bars

not encountered since the last

chapter

      Gluten free pornography

contorts a wild stab

at a world of impossible unions

further encounters

behind the bleachers, a destination

of impeccable mnemonic locus

When just down the hall

the penny drops

and the shoe's on the other

foot, satisfaction descends in flurried

understanding, that special clarity

available from rationed ratios

and rationalizations wrapped up

in ribbons of alliterative laughter

once again makes an appearance

as truth

or dare

operational on levels of onto-

foolery leave the stakes fading

into the background

        So who's

to say what's carried in the wind's

belly, or nursed by the earth? who

will stand for obscure idioms

beyond discursive boxes' reasoned

take on paradise's primal lingo?

And if heaven *no longer flutters*

except exsanguinate and grimacing

circulation jests with it, cheeky

unafraid of toes left throbbing

by clumsy digressions, gravity's

pull on boxes of clichés designed

to grease wheels and increase

completion's hold on heaven's

remnant
                    Oranges, sunny

rooms and cockatoos fail

to hit the spot but offer

lyrical solicitude, though gluten

content is reportedly high

                              A peignoir

however, suggests that *porné*

is never far from the poem's

often melodious determinations

while graphic dimensions

waver on the edge of obscure

vocabularies, fold

after fold of sweet

meat and healthy considerations

of tumescent excitement's

cosmographical disturbance

circulates through multiple

spheres of entangled disparate

vision leaves lust thankfully

desiccated and demoted except

in quarters designated heritage

sites for people who confuse

fundament for anatomical extension

into spiritual contraction's tight

puckered state of stick penetration

and containment frenzy

One Cup Of This (Before Bed) Burns Belly Fat Like Crazy. **TEFolin** contains the naturally occurring ingredient, **HYDROXYCITCRIC ACID**, which BOOSTS WEIGHT LOSS by **BLOCKING EXCESS BODY FAT** production while ☛INCREASING RESTING METABOLISM☛ by more than 130%. This combination makes the body go from a fat-gain to fat-loss state !!while resting!!. Never lift a finger again and look just like Brangelina. Eat to your swollen heart's content and become more and more slim and attractive, more IRRESISTIBLE with every bite you shove in your pie hole and you never have to do anything (DO NOTHING!!!) but shovel it in and watch the pounds **drop off** it's so easy you don't have to do anything you can kick back and watch reruns of The Apprentice knowing the **HYDROXYCITCRIC ACID**, that miracle of modern science, that precious gift of the Enlightenment, is working away erasing EVERY CALORIE (yes, you heard that right—Every Calorie) of that enormous meatball sub you are forcing down your engorged throat freeing you from the burden of effort and releasing you into the bliss of unrestrained consumption and gluten free pornography.

Gluten-free pornography besides belly fat

speech acts is the myth beyond us drowns

us in a sea of sense in recesses of Perfection's

seduction where cruelty dwells, immense

deathless, brooking no dissent, no thinking

beyond proscription, no darkness unembraced

children ripped

from mothers'

& fathers' arms

can't compete with the laughter

accompanies it

for sheer soulless jubilation, a strange

word to find here where joy glows

with angelic input, not this celebration

of pain, one might say the devil's

work leaves soul in the tightening web

of 14th century chuckles

over interdicted kindness, conscript

prescript, proscribed drive

scribe's connected script

restricted in proscriptive

phantasmagoria of dropped c's for t's

or some other *letter flux*, shiny

pieces ticking along in pain's projection

blessed form locked down

somewhere between doghouse

and do-gooder by displaced

lust for control till the first

encounter with poetry, always on

oblivion's edge, spreads vivacious

turmoil's terminal indeterminations

leaves dogma whimpering at the door

A gluten-free origin myth

When Louie Z incarnates
as Mother's Body trouble waits
when young Prometheus agitates
for his tone deaf reading

Then Daddy Dunk's bump and blather
leaves Prometheus all a lather
indignation's endless natter
gushing and gushing

Young Prometheus waxes irate
spinning tales of murderous doom fate
Daddy's acts of brutal hate
just bumping and yelling

Ideology, Young Prom declares
to be the true and rightful heir
Meaning's latest avatar
in Zizek's ridiculous signage

Chorus cries be nice, the stakes are nada

this is the same old enchilada

full of pointless, picky dada

calumniations

They bitch and moan of bully tactics

meanwhile using systematic

imposed silence, & made up facts it

promulgates

But purloined records finally freed

from Young P's desperate clutch and greed

show Daddy Dunk's simple need

for a sense of fun

Daddy Dunk speaks from the grave

how YP's lost in Plato's cave

divorced from human meaning gave

us the world

Heavens roar and seas recede

in overdetermined causality

the poem needs when planting the seed

of mythic structure

Young Prom and Daddy Dunk fight on

thru climes reserved in old eons

for figures imagination won

from Eternity

Uncertain pornography rocks forth

and back, fro and to, out

and in, seeks balance flesh offers

flesh, where Olson took it, poised

against weight and tally of each ounce

of rendered human fat, turning

to the impossibility of it

    talking meat / scribbling flesh

A True Pornographic Myth Based on an Uncertain Story

Sun and Moon

hot to get it on, hot

for flesh on stiffening flesh, slipping

flesh in flesh around

flesh, hot, wet

engorged flesh

so they beat it

after Earth's wedding to Sky

headed

lickety split to Earth's vacant

domicile, hot to get in, lips

touch, hands brush

clothing aside, swollen

flesh, fumble

with the Key but

Lock won't yield

won't give up

its entrance

Key can't enter

                                        through its crossed

                                        legs, surprise obstruction

reeks of mythic knots analog

to path's fated rupture

                    So Moon

steps up as Sun jimmies the window

takes his foot in her gentle hands

                                and boosts

                                        Sun through

                                                        and into

Earth's house where he rushes

to clear the Obstacle

                        and Moon enters

                        through the freed door

                        into the house of love's

                        passionate touch

                        returns story

                        to the path assures flesh

of the knowledge

that it's common

And they tumble

into the Bedroom

head over heels

Moon and Sun a tangle

of limbs, flesh against flesh, insistent

flesh slick with *anxious secretions*

from secret, holy places

entrance breached, window

jimmied, Moon boosted Sun

with gentle cupped hands, and they

found the Bedroom

where they suddenly knew

they were in

the Wrong House

not Earth's House, a Stranger's House

transgressed by Sun and Moon driven

senseless by flesh, they jimmied the window

passed through the Law, thieves

in the night caught in the net

of hot flesh they went through

the wrong window, found themselves

naked

on a Stranger's bed

The *Window* is a myth of variable outcome

depending on prepositional placement

                              From a different angle

it also has surplus value

                    an ideological

observation on the foundation

of the current Oligarchy

but irrelevant in determinations

of further vision

                    When prepositions

relocate, the window may or may not

become symbolic in which case it's lost

to itself and must haunt far reaches of discourse

in quest of a way *in*, which, as everyone knows

with windows goes *out*, too, collapsing frames

of reorientation within shaky regimes

of uncertain focus bred mystery

reveals apparition escaped

some leaky textual lock up

to show up here, radiant

in an ordinary kind of way

(*burnished corn's idea of the sun*)

and slips by the window as prepositional

matrix nursed spatial vertigo falls

into story's every which way

        Form unfolds from actual

        spiritual ordeal, intrepid travel

        in multiple zones through realms

        of intuition's mission

        the poem born from

        knowledge, ear's

        attention to perpetual

        brilliant question hovers

        just beyond the last word

        living on the edge

                of health

                of poverty

                of city

                of order

                of sky

                                        of mind–

                        [News of encounters

                        with further apparitions of further

                        worlds sounding

                        off the coast of today]

Within the cosmic Arch, role distribution

proceeds in orders Random

finds confusing and Uncertain

still seeking a stable level

of signification identifies as your usual

familial dysfunction passing

for normal mythic violence

in the name of obedience

                                Jimmy the window

for instance, outlawed

by the Doom Program

whose architects in eternity

have weighted the dice darkly—

[Having abandoned all to Program's

modulated misery—*lane bound*

and *stuck behind*—(orange blossoms'

smudge pots, familiar disaster's

greasy residue on the window

sill) beyond which Eros and Thanatos

tangle in a bedroom

farce, apparitions of confused

but unthwarted desire

lounging on the beach

of destiny's farthest reach

in manifest desolation and mortal

sin, missing the mark by a country

mile meanders through divagating

syntax to deflect arrival

at eschaton's obvious

damnation waiting amid ruins

of history for its moment in the rising sun]

            Rising on what? Uncertain mutters

            mentally ticking off

            cruelties currently drop

            from sun drenched sky

on *a* school,

a hospital

a home

where

a father

wails

dead daughter dangling

from his arms

**Poem beginning and ending with lines
from Jay Wright's "Three Pots Figure a Going
and a Return"**

The Bay *treats me kindly* spreads

glassy morning's smooth clarity

plays with mind cradled distance

out where edge slices sky

Reflected depths leaden gray

extends past island's intimate limit –

leave at 11, turn off water, gas up

then drive and other forms of *entangled*

Reminded by stones left

behind mile high ice gouged retreat

in recesses just off shore where lightless

lucid marks chiaroscuro transit

The depth of each *cell* offers dark

vistas beyond island's frame into death's

mystery, sweep beyond prepositional

goad to evade finitude's sweet *end*

Textures of morning's air, strange currents

shift across kaleidoscope face,

hieroglyphic dance picks up with the wind

quiet tumult of *flickersense*

Says *Love's breath is spare* & smells of ice

in March when water & stone whisper

a wild logos known to murmur

in the wake of its unsettled touch

Jimmie the window, break

into Stranger's place

unsanctioned muss

transgressed bed's

alien duvet, unafraid

of gluten's occult influence

on bellies and other repositories

of mysterious *porné* accumulations,

yield to flesh, hot wet

mindflesh

The end that's coming is not

the same as the one

outlined in the manual

                The arrow of time

                missed the mark

in the dark of the moon

whose light, though not original

glows through tunes

of archeological significance

You can't know the date

without the soundtrack

and while the chain

of events relies on intervening

angel's hands, the links

may or may not glow with it

                Then you are there

                way up in the blue

with Thelma and Lou, the edge

a great wonder, their constellation

rising in the east, mythic marker

arrayed star dance

                in imagination's sky

Chapter 9

Introduction to random

"Let's go."

—Virgil to Dante, *Inferno,* Canto IV

In cosmic architecture patched together

by the current Regime of Certain Cruelty

(Evil Orange Clown Division) random names roam

one hundred billion galaxies

looking for meanings might cover

senseless imposition of pain, or instant

temporal amnesia, random metamorphoses

of off the wall stupidities, ever-shifting *you*

buried beneath habitual tumulus

and aggravated Typhonic space fissure

rejectamenta

Uncertain, witness to random

excitations of the underlying field

prefers theorizing social graces

even as interminable perturbation's

barely detectable indices of matrix's slip

from zone to zone with no regard

for proper orientation raises the question

what do strange attractors

and morphological goals

have to do with Cinvat Bridge?

                    It's uncertain

the answer's uncertain, the Angel left to fend

for itself in a long fade to black,

and likely susceptible to random

hook ups with sleazy non-sequiturs

and punk digressions lead to promiscuous

speculation on the abandoned cuckoo's

ability to find home and your

average border collie's

                    love of beauty

            Biting off

            more than you can chew

            is a possible outcome

            of a blank page

            in orders of coherent

            development, age being

            what it is and the demand

for product acceptable

to some peaked imagination

of an empire of art, Virgil

without gods, beating the drum

for uninterrupted personal greatness

an immobilized state of eternal

victory, arms raised, roars

of adulation, laurel

pouring out the wazoo

                        More than you can chew

signifies the *other* side of the island

just offshore, holds together edges

of the world in semblance of troubled

order, white crash against stones

in a non-Straussian sound track

to its own thoughtless "violence"

                            This side too

when you chew

more than you can bite

and September wind contracts

exposed flesh leaves letters' awkward

scrawl on the page of its record

to be deciphered some later time

already written and/or un

written

      Hence, the *more*

biting and chewing and/or chewing

and biting in the midst of roar's

turbulence, *humiliating in its disguises,*

crushing absence a part of game's

rules, do not pass go, do not collect

the final word of its curl and crash

watermusic's crescendo, swell

and break and

swell

in this arranged

          investment of love

evens the ground even as Doom

Program's avatars wrench a breach

in cosmic decorum leads to contractions

of available sources of giving and circulatory

access, clogging the works

and invading Ukraine

          Slipping into time

and space as wrought in the Waiting

Room's interminable silence, *tarrying*

with the formal expenditure of the given

makes no claim on stabilized

matrices or other attempts at intergalactic

positioning but expand from deep

in mismatched hiatus, this cork board

perplexity where a calm sea butts vaguely

against privacy policy, mountain

pure water and rhetoric's ghost

We interrupt our regular poetry programming to bring you this

Emergency Bulletin

Late last night Authorities issued an Emergency Bulletin seeking information as to the current whereabouts of the *Anima Mundi* whose disappearance is thought to be connected to the current ShutDown which has drastically restricted worldwide circulatory energies. Witnesses report last seeing her enter the Emergency Department at the Cosmic Centre for Addiction and Mental Health (CCAMH), although no one at CCAMH has been able to clarify whether she was a patient or a visitor, or even if she was there at all.

Conflicting reports as to her state of mind shortly before she disappeared have clouded the situation. Some unofficial Soul Watchers have insisted that she looked despondent and was possibly a danger to herself. Officials from the Administration, however, immediately dismissed suggestions she was suffering from terminal depression. "She's fine," Chief Rump stated. "Never looked better. I grabbed her by . . . I mean I *saw* her . . . that's what I said, I *saw* her less than an hour ago and she told me this was far and away the best Administration ever. Ever. She also told me what a great Administrator I am, the best Administrator she has ever seen. And, by the way, I never said Mexico would pay for it."

Close associates of the missing anima expressed fear for her well-being and suggested a general soul shutdown was inevitable. "The last 3 or 4 years have been particularly hard on her," *Unus Mundus* told investigators. "I worry she may have hurt herself, she was so despondent over the toxic Mean Streak fouling the *Mundi Imaginalis* with its disgusting black goo. She threatened to throw herself into the jaws of that massive Fence-cavator poised on the southern border."

Others, however, discounted reports of *Anima Mundi*'s suicidal despair as the cause of her disappearance. *Paranatman* pointed to the recent outbreak of multiple Typhonic fissures in the S/T Connective Fabric as a more logical culprit. A long-time observer of Interdimensional Stability Grids, *Paranatman* thinks that the recent successive waves of *ClogD anti-energy** alone were enough to account for the weakness of her signal. Add the mass *NecroMental* [n]G broadcasts from last week's Typhonic Fear rupture and there's more than enough congealed darkness to have swallowed her up as she strolled through some mythic meadow gathering flowers with friends and attendants, thus precipitating The ShutDown."

No one seems able to agree on the long term effects of the Shutdown but people with knowledge of previous cosmic closures suggest the future may be glimpsed in the culture of certain gated communities in Florida where general *Souldeath* is required in one of the codicils to the White Master Codex along with an uninterrupted supply of Barry Manilow muzak and *big honkin'* t-bones with potatoes. And golf.

---

*See John Clarke, *Tramping the Bulrushes.*

Random incursions continue

to disturb compositional satisfaction

with occasional bad rhymes

and news from tomorrow's

scrawl *leaves* autumn to fall

where it may though rough

winds and darling buds

belong to another part

of speech, their presence, a concept

not unfamiliar with the inside

of a ring, is welcome here

where errant homonymies

punch holes in a sentence

without parole, a slip even more

translinguistically, you could say

hot, in today's parlance, opening

as it does, channels or maybe

little canals, in any case, across

Atlantic's swell to arrive

at a body resonant with meaning

crucible's resin burning

fragrant still through all

those years of *to leave*

  Meanwhile

stuck behind violates velocity's

freedom expectations, double yellow blues

creeping behind Road Lord's monstrous

apparition surges down asphalt sock

oblivious to small existences below

and uncertain outcomes a quarter

inch variance (mined in Brazil

shipped to China, turned into a part,

parts from Mexico and Lexington,

assembled in Brampton) makes,

and if it slips—oops—or the Road Lord

misjudges the turn and the one

coming the other way slips gently

into the ditch to miss him

the driver hauling on the wheel

then pops out

                        across the road

                                    gibbous waxing

                                              death grill

                                                        looms

Stuck behind, the daily habit of stalled

lives in carbon monoxide clouds

turned into a sitting duck

a soon to be random

distribution of formerly

composed cells known as *Jim*

                    (When Uncertain first noticed

Random, she was sitting in a café

near the intersection of x and y, small world

Uncertain thought, just when I was about

to call on faith to explain the Big Yellow

Truck hurtling across the road

bearing oblivion, driver's eyes far

above, god-like, wide with doom

knowledge, a quarter inch

suddenly looks like an angel)

            But wait cried a voice

from beyond the margins, Random and Fate

are late arrivals to the party

of bewildered drivers, bewildered

heroes, and a quarter of an inch is the name

Random gives to numbers' magic fabric

binds disparate points in its web, where three to one

is still an arena of unknown distributions

and meaning has its own sensorium

>   The way
>
>   down Doom Road
>
>   starts with Seven
>
>   (come)
>
>   Eleven
>
>   a brown bag
>
>   wrapped Bud
>
>   Big Boy
>
>   and ends *inter alia*
>
>   the stately
>
>   redwoods lit
>
>   by a fireball

Doom Road's antics are measured

in random quarter inch discriminations

of death, the Big Yellow Truck,

capitalized, is no metaphor

much less symbol

Neither is *Stuck*

Behind when attempting to exit

the setup determined in distant

indeterminations of boxed

cats and other continuums

of destiny's inescapable quarter

inch—in the rear view

mirror the guy behind sees

it coming, his eyes grow, Jim

was his name and still is

in these lines' random acknowledgements

of mirrored surprise, *driving*

north at 4:40 P.M. when Billy,

he of the doom knowledge,

had to whip his steering wheel

and *three back wheels slipped*

off the road and the rest

is the story of a quarter

of an inch

and a fireball

Random is as random does says Harvey

appearing out of the blue

                      If the words out

of the blue seem to refer to the word sky

where is it and how deep

is the ocean?

            This way he says

with a slight toss of his head, blue

then, as a variation on eternity

a flash of starlight

in your lover's eye

Meanwhile, talk of random spreads

through Uncertain's social circle, infects

miscellaneous with a noun like affliction

leaves it unsure of its place

in the sentence spreads out

toward some new combination

of verbal contingency disguised

as the distribution of border guards

When the bones settle in the bottom

of night's bowl who will be the number

one pick for entrance qualified

by stormy Monday—

7 come 11

Get out of the kitchen

if you can't stand the heat is a logical

destination, though sometimes confused

and unable to find useful reference

overdetermined causality brings

to the Great Good Housekeeping

Seal of Approval

Determined efforts

of the Doom Program to eliminate

all pockets of resistance through ongoing

operations sow seeds of exclusion,

acquisition, possession, the three

Graces of its insatiable clutch

necessary anodynes, having ceded

the ground to machine death's

                         program outcomes

                         Not knowing

what comes next may seem

random, but despite signs

of sense, *randomsense* also spreads

across white stubbled fields

with seasonal units of joy

exaltation and intermittent

bursts of advertising leave

the whole thing trembling

in indeterminate modes

of precipitation

                  The Big Yellow Truck

may be a sign of vibratory formation

sometimes mistaken for *identity*

in modulations of water, a sign too

of random as a dream of entrance

through a jimmied window

into splendor beyond the Law

                                    Absent a sense

of humour, irony stands in for laughter's

raucous leveling, a smirk of the known

in the place of judgement

                                    Jimmie the window

                                    Harvey says

peering around a corner

                                    looking cryptic

                                    Let's go

Harvey, I barely knew you, the poem says

That's okay, Harvey says.

I did too.

Chapter 10
Leaving 2, including a Special Section on Leaving Art

"The basis of all metrical determination must be sought outside the manifold in the binding forces which act on it."

—Bernhard Riemann

Current Typhonic Onset's

significant encroachments

on territories recently secured

for circulatory exactitude and precise

compassion has led

to ensuing enclosures

recall

    the fall

        of beer

into totalitarian hops regimes

in the wake of Unum Wave's

colonizing displacement of Whole

into One, banning heather

and wormwood in the name

of *Whole-some* imposition

of bitterness whose hops coincidentally owned and distributed

by the same Lordly lawmakers

doling out regiments of armed ~~Soldiers~~

Sales Representatives to continents

underrepresented by white

engineers and bankers and in need

of IPA

    thus initiating the chain

of events leads inevitably

to the current sad inundation

of grapefruit flavoured beer

    Back to leaving should not come

out of the dark after this further

interruption of sense and push

toward a gain on form arising

from a shift of obedience

                left longing

for history, art, mom, community

democracy, autonomous and other

tattered remains of the last mass

Phantasy's haunting coherence

                    To leave

the old cave, they say, requires

insurrection, violence of *to rise*

or *Arise!* against localized necrotic infarction

intrudes on leaving's circulation

Then we are off to the traces

though the question remains

have we gotten anywhere?

                              Leaving

the gate would suggest otherwise

given popularity of coliseums'

ovoid evidence in gathering spots

scattered across ancient

textual guides to ghost

world leaves leaving to stagger—

a word unjustly connected

to roadside failure—into unsuspected

quotes: "It gives me great pleasure,

my daughter, to write to you,

although I have nothing

to tell you" (Madame de Sevigné,

via J-L Nancy)

It would help

if Direction would clarify

its status if not actual bearings

so that descent could orient

leaving in a meaningful arrangement

of words (each an event of unique

discontinuity lacking discretion

to distance itself from fables

of interior

        I can't go on past *once*

upon a time unless leaving

goes, too, so that *already* is just

a matter of random intervention

in old scrawl's unfolding

happenstance as it wanders

following the dog's perfect

indication of unspeakable

sensorium's rich whim and inevitable

confrontation pursues scent

through virtual Andes of layered

greetings, fragrant graffiti, lives

narrated palimpsests of sprayed

stories endless exemplar, *gnosis*

of not knowing, or knowing

as leaving

Leaving is sometimes coming

in ways the poem

couldn't foresee, How

did you get here

it wants to know, and Where

is it? Instances abound, instants

too, unruly homonymies disrupt

dimensional discretion leaving

coming as in *coming*

home and no one can see you

What's left wonders

at infrangible facture, later's

Whitejacket knowledge, porous

borders, slippery selves, creation's

con

    What you leave

is not what's left—palm trees,

orange blossom ghost, desert sunrise

with Death & James from a rock pool

in its heart the day

before leaving

       and arriving is no

guarantee you're there, Helen

walks by, patchouli brush, Saturday

Burrard sidewalk surge

of warm flesh, breasts hardened

nipples below brown eyes, last

winter's *before* shattered neck's

shorn shaved wraith her brown eyes see

nothing, open on No One, invisible

returned skeletal shade, a memory

where No One walks the street

of somewhere

        ('You!' said the Caterpillar contemptuously.

        'Who are you?')

They went into the mountains at night and practiced strange rites.

        Passing through leaves explication

        to local representative

        tour guide's navigation

        through narrow conjunctions

        crowded modifiers dangling

        from dismantled scaffolds

        at the edge of the adjective

        dump but having passed

        through Winnemucca is not enough

        to qualify as leaving since arriving

        is its two step jig, its holding

        on and letting go phantasia

        of emergent new world

        syllabic stumble

into first sounds'

abyss of sense

                      Themis

           Harvey mutters

           from the cloud of unknowing

           on the front porch

                       Ice

           glints beyond his concern

           for law's order, home's

           ways etched in forms

           No One sees in her

           eyes passing by

           rather than through

           a distinction the surge

           doesn't know—which differs

           from unknowing's long

           time flirtation with Uncertain—

           rolling up the windows, so

           to speak, when driving through

           or close to sections

           of the poem designated

           bad neighbourhoods

in orderly distribution

of arrival's program

No One leaves

when they wants to, when

the Big Rig comes the other

way, spreads enormous wings

signals *indivisible punctuality,*

when the vague Bridge emerges

from cinematic mist

punctuated by haloed glow

of Border checkpoint's

muted illumination out

of the night

Leaving is also behind, a late

preposition in this formation's

indices, heart's malfunction, a rear view

mirror framing abandoned's

pit in neat parallelogram depth

'I can't explain myself, I'm afraid, sir' said Alice, 'because I'm not myself, you see.'

What's a trace & who's departed

they demand to know

at the Border where coming

& leaving look like Katherine

Hepburn & Spencer Tracy

in *State of the Union*, no Polly

Wolly Doodle marriage for them

corrupted phoneme by phoneme

by the filth of money and power

Capra beginning to see

the darkness

for what it was, who had won

America from sea to oil

slicked sea, not an inconsequential

reference given current configuration

of KleNched & KloGged, sub

sub routines of the Doom

Program's general lock

down, or, say, *Button Down*

although fashion's vicissitudes

may have sucked the punch

out of that one depending on

button's current sign status

in the *Identommodities* Market

or its Signification Valence Strength

in micro-*musthaves*, wearable

assurances that all is well

and help is on the way

LEAVING ART
A FEW POINTERS

Leaving art is easy

as 1, 2, 3 . . . or 11 Steps to Success

anyone with determined spirit

and a few simple tools

can do it

      Just ask Cecilia Gimenez,

famed restorer of Christ images

      When the 500 year old

      Ecce Homo fresco

      in the Sanctuary of Mercy

      her local church in Borja

      showed signs of wear and tear

      Cecilia didn't ask who could help

      she grabbed some brushes left

      from the last kitchen reno

      ran to the church

      and went to work leaving

                Art behind

        Yes!!!

It's really that easy, just follow

11 Steps to Success

in our easy to read, up-dated

fully modernized, shiny

all inclusive

Leaving Art package

Just $19.99

But our story doesn't end there . . .

Cecilia, hot with success

rewarded herself with a well

deserved holiday, but when she returned

was outraged to find her work

all over Social Media

where it was lampooned

                  ridiculed

                        and mocked

by elites and masses alike

                  But before Cecilia

could defend herself, blessed

saints intervened, turned the situation

in her favour when her post-art

masterpiece got so many "Likes"

it became the object

of pilgrimage

by devout Pilgrims who don't care

what they look at so long as something

is there, something the book

says people should look

at

Desperate for somewhere

to go, something to look at

multitudes flock to Borja where they enter

the irony of god's sad demise

with passion, an eye for a good deal

and an utter lack of understanding

of their deicidal guilt and stare

absent even feigned interest

at what's on the wall

A multitude we can guarantee *you*

and your post-art career if you just follow

11 Steps to Success detailed

in our world acclaimed manual

Leaving Art

a mere $19.99

But trouble brewed in paradise

Cecilia's post-art (Re)Fresco

became Beloved, drawing crowds so huge

and hungry for post-art (or anything

really, pizza gelato Botticelli) that her church

                                            began to charge

                                            an Entrance Fee

That's not the trouble, though

even if it is the same old

moneychanger in the temple

bullshit, no, the trouble was

they wouldn't split the take

with Cecilia, wouldn't

cut her in on the scam

After getting the news,

Mrs. Gimenez got hip

and lawyered up

She's the one

fucked it up in the first place

her mouthpiece announced

She deserves a cut, she just

wants the church

to obey the law

(which one?

Uncertain wondered)

In response the Church

lawyered up, too

Dealing with lawyers is crucial

to our 11 Steps to Success

in a post-art world, a world where art

just doesn't cut it, doesn't

make sense anymore so step

into your future

leave your old life behind

become a Post-Art Celeb

a virtual

god

and all it takes

is one small payment

$19.99, and you too will

Leave Art

and make your very own

Ecce Homo

                                        Leaving is the first note out

                                        of silence, each first sound

                                        departure to departure sings

                                        exactitude of impossible

                                        measure

Dogwood blush

through brown con

fusion, white hush

stranger it

comes, leaves

of words

thin crisp skin

crunch across swell

of arrival leaves

breath clouds

precipitate drift

punctuates announcement's

brute silence

untold flicker

of tangle and flurry

Optative *If* breed's No One

modality's way of being verbs

without substantives, if only

Uncertain can find a way

to mind its manners while falling

into *linguistic nomadism*'s

unquiet circling and circling

(snakes they said, deep in cells

where memory dwells) toward no

settled leaving

www.ingramcontent.com/pod-product-compliance
Lightning Source LLC
Chambersburg PA
CBHW011215120626
46545CB00008B/2997